The Adoption Tree

Written & Illustrated by
Kimberly James

Copyright © 2017 Kimberly James
All rights reserved.

ISBN: 1533126631
ISBN-13: 978-1533126634

The Adoption Tree

Written & Illustrated by
Kimberly James

DEDICATION

To Caleb and Will,

May you not only know how much we love you,
but how much God loves you.
I pray that you continue to see that God planted
you in the perfect spot!

Jeff,
I am so honored to do life with you! You are the greatest
Husband and Father, and we are so blessed to call you ours!

There once was this little seedling growing in a yard.

God loved this little seedling and knew him by name because he created him.

God had big plans for him.

One day, God told this little seedling that he would not stay in the spot where he was growing.

You see, it wasn't the best spot for him to fully grow into what God knew he could be.

The soil wasn't just right, as it didn't quite have the nutrients to make him tall and strong.

He also wasn't in a spot where the sun could give him the warmth and security that he really needed to grow into the tree God knew he could be.

So the little seedling was carefully dug up and handled with care.

Even though it was sad for the little seedling to know it wasn't going to grow in that spot, he knew God loved him and wanted what was best for him.

So, he trusted that God knew what He was doing.

God planted him in a new spot, perfectly chosen for him.

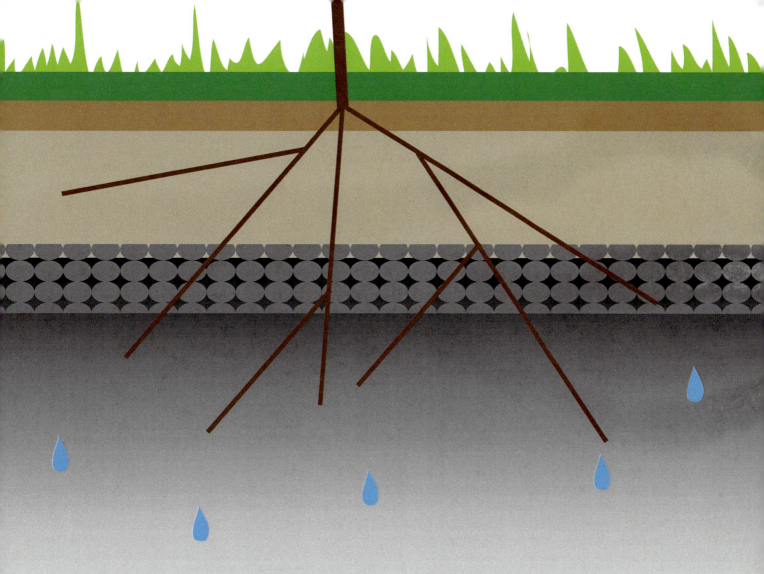

The little seedling immediately felt how the soil was just right. It felt so soft and squishy. His roots were able to grow down deep which allowed him to get water even when it didn't rain. He also realized that as he grew taller, his branches could stretch as far as they needed to go.

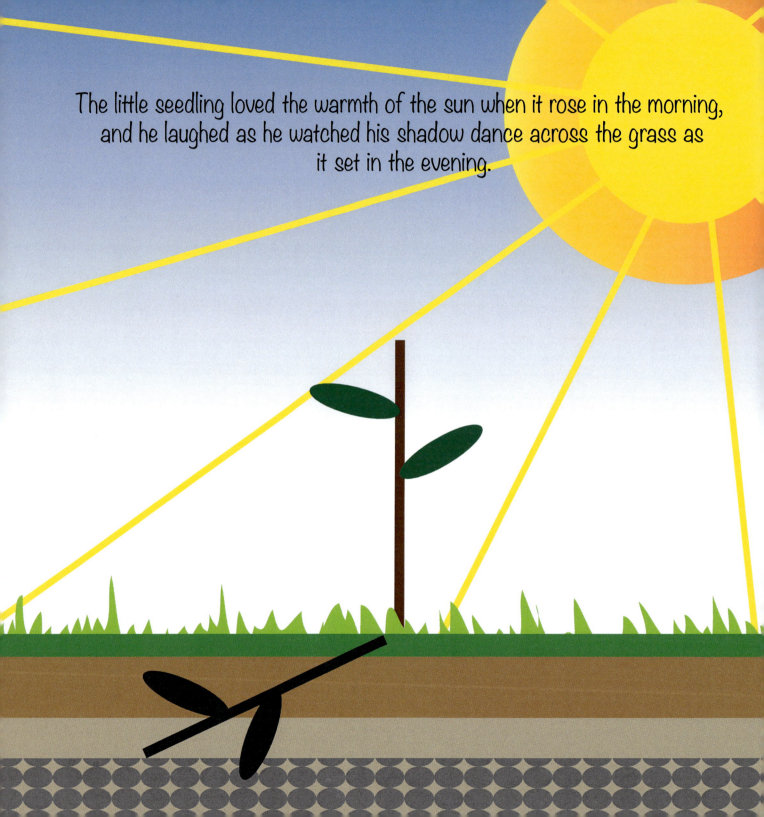

He was overjoyed to see that it was the perfect spot!

He thanked God for planting him there to grow.

And grow is what he did!

He grew tall and strong with his branches stretching way out, and as he grew, he learned that God had a special purpose for him. He realized that where he used to grow, he wouldn't have been able to carry out his special purpose.

He learned that his branches could be a home for birds building their nests, and also a perfect place for them to perch and sing.

Different bugs such as lady bugs and butterflies also enjoyed climbing his limbs to feed on the beautiful green leaves he provided.

He even saw that as he grew, his leaves could provide shade for those who wanted to have a picnic.

His branches were even strong enough to hold a swing.

You see little one, you are just like this tree.
God has big plans for you too!

You once were growing inside your birthmother as a true gift from God.

After you were born, God knew you wouldn't stay with her. She was not able to provide what you needed to be what God knew you were going to be.

You were created especially for our family, and God planted you with us.

Adopted into our family!

God knew that in our family, you would be able to grow into who He created you to be.

He created each person in our family in a special way knowing that we would all perfectly fit together!

And boy, was He right! You are absolutely perfect for us!

May you remember, little one...

God loves you and always wants what is best for you.
Trust God with what he has done with your life,
and may you be like this little tree...

...overjoyed to see that you are in the perfect spot!!!

ABOUT THE AUTHOR

We started out our adoption process in October 2009. At that same time, my dad gave us a little seedling to plant in our yard. I didn't realize it at the time, but my husband said that he always thought of this little tree as our adoption tree. We planted it at the time when adoption was planted in our hearts, and as it grew, our love and faith in an adoption grew as well. This tree was to signify our child and be a way to help explain adoption...of how a little seedling from one yard, was brought and planted into our yard and raised...just like our child through an adoption.

Well, we didn't know it at the time, but God was showing us through this little tree what He had up His sleeve for us. Our little tree split into two that summer...with one branch growing a little taller than the other...signifying our little twin boys...Caleb (Baby A) was a lot bigger than Will (Baby B). God is so good!!! His hands have been all over our adoption, and He even used a little tree to show my husband and I that he hears our prayers, and has blessed us beyond what we could ever imagine.

Made in the USA
Monee, IL
28 October 2020